Mitsumasa Anno

# ANNO'S MATH GAMES II

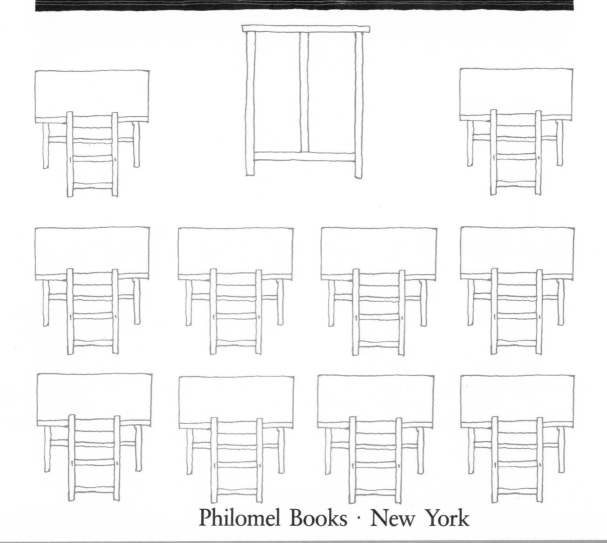

Philomel Books · New York

# · 1 ·

# The Magic Machine

Kriss and Kross have invented a wonderful magic machine. They've just finished working on it. Their machine has two openings. If something is put into the opening on the left, it comes out as something different on the right.

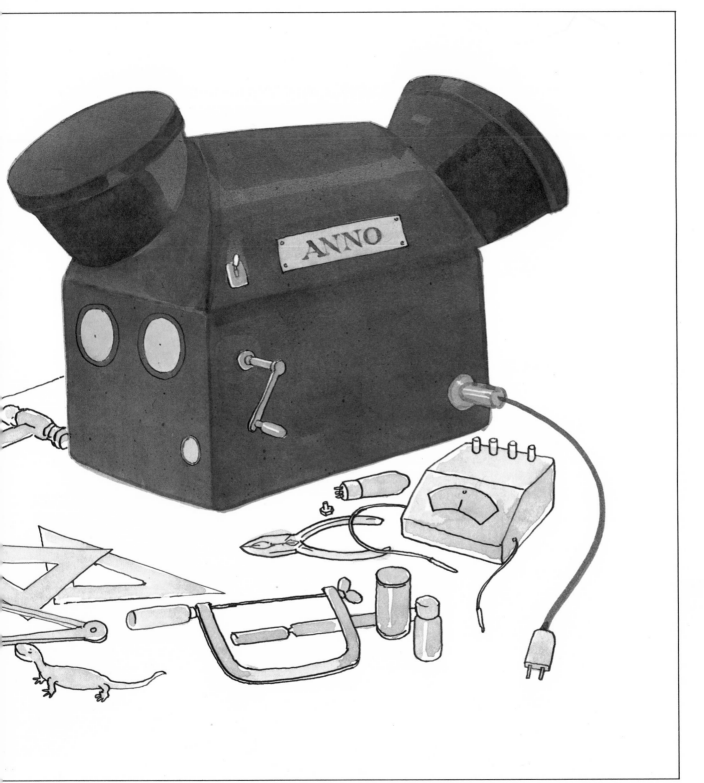

Our friends are putting in a pair of glasses now. Surprise! A pair of glasses with eyes comes out of the other side.

If the things on the left page are put in, they come out looking like the things on the right page. What would you call a machine that works this way?

Now they've changed the controls on
the machine. What has it done this
time? And what do you suppose would
happen if they put the small chicken
into the right opening, instead of the left?

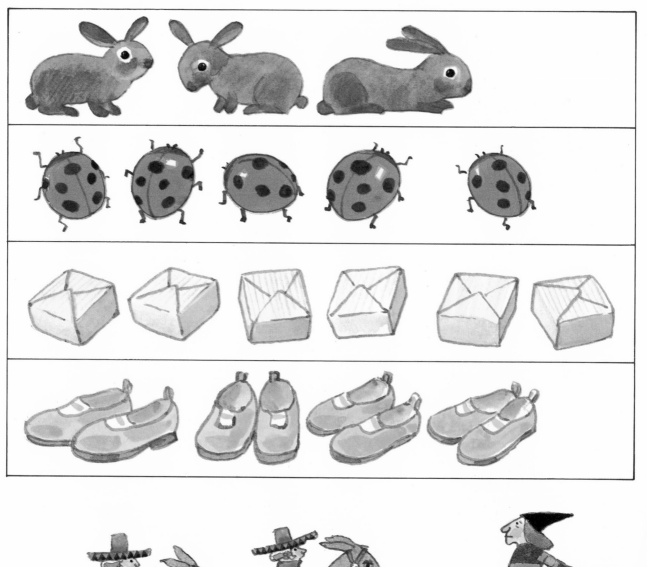

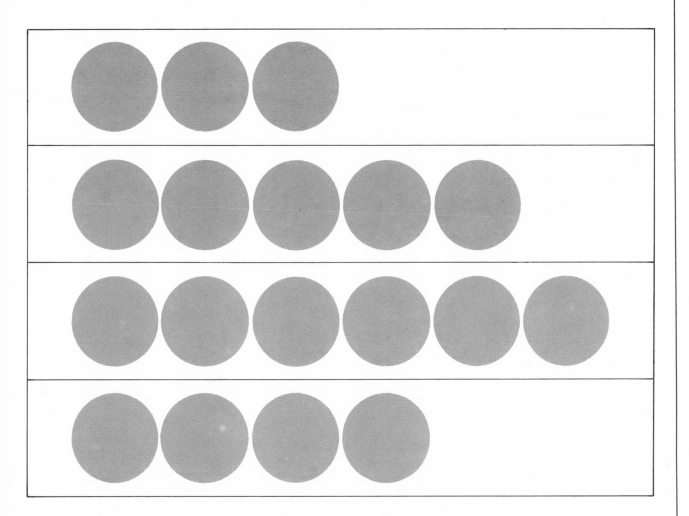

Two cowboys have come riding up on mules. They say that they want to get into this machine. What would happen to them? Kriss and Kross have shut the lid on the right. Now nothing can enter the machine from the right side. What can get out?

The controls on the machine have been changed again. What in the world is it doing now?

Now Kross is putting in four glasses of juice. What are going to come out?

Here's one that's not too difficult. But notice that the lid on the right is down again. Can you figure out why?

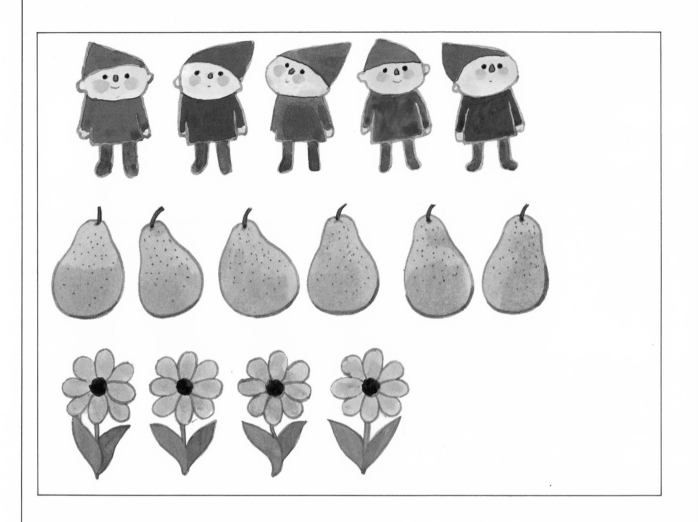

Compare the left and right pages and
think carefully about what is happening.
Our friends are putting six dragonflies
into the right side. What will come out?
What will happen if they put the remaining
dragonflies into the right side again?

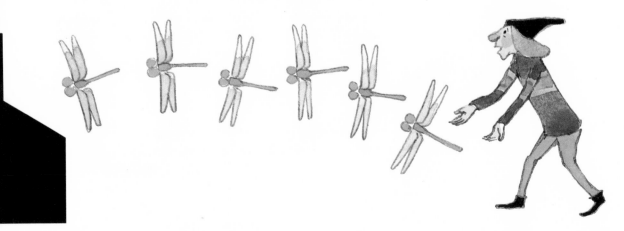

Uh-Oh! They used the machine so much that it finally broke down. Does your head ever feel all confused and muddled like that?

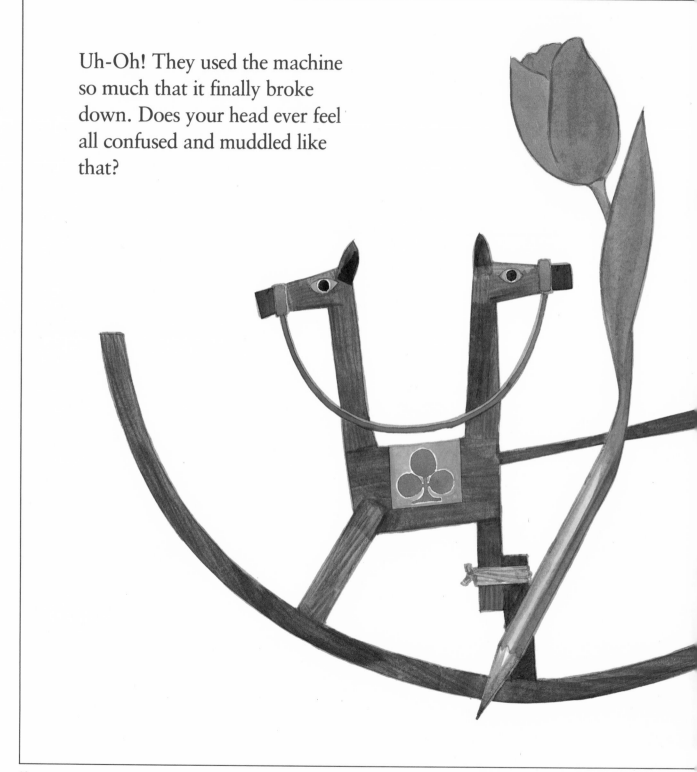

# ·2·

# Compare and Find Out

Here are two dolls. Are
these two pictures of the
same doll, or are they
two different dolls? Let's
compare them carefully.

Look at the shapes of the
faces and the bodies.
And what about the hats
and clothes? Let's com-
pare one thing at a time.

Let's compare these two pictures. You can see that both are dogs. How many ears does each dog have? How are the ears shaped?

Now take a look at these two pictures. They're not exactly the same, but they look the same, don't they? What's the same and what's different?

From here on, you can think on your own.
The more closely you look, the more things
you can find that are the same, and that are
different.

31

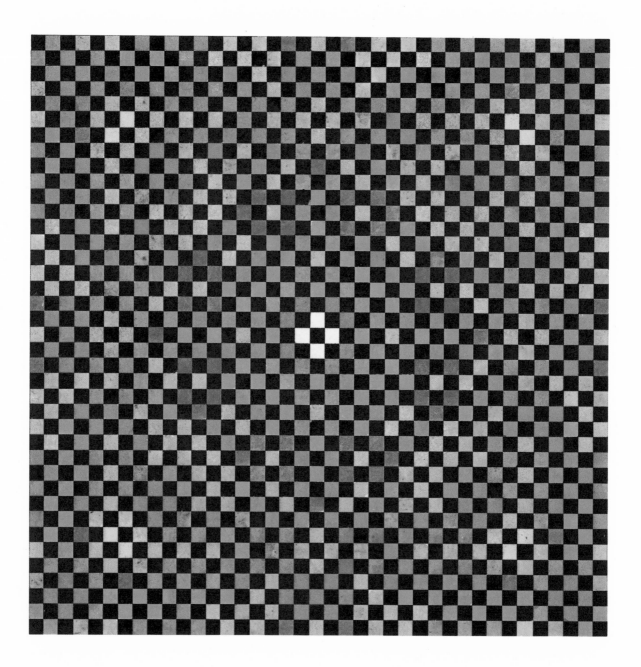

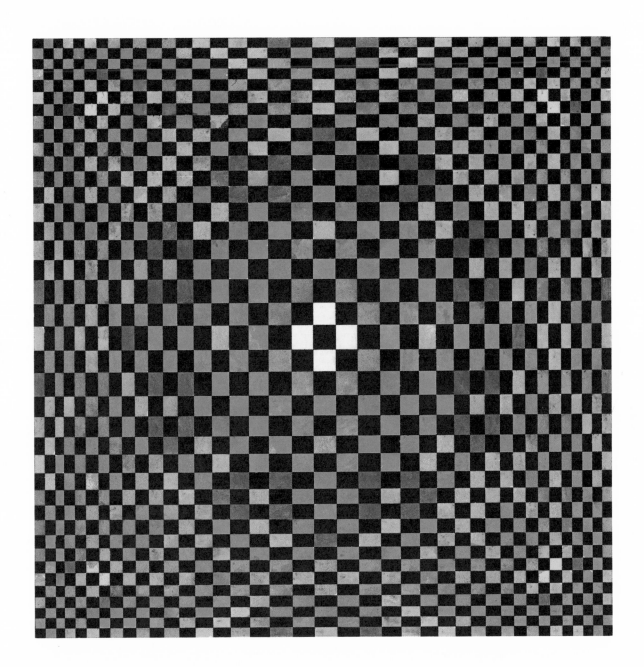

# · 3 ·

## Dots, Dots, and More Dots

Our little friend, Kriss, is running the sewing machine. Click, click, each stitch is connected together. From a distance, the stitches seem like one long line. The holes of the stamp look like a line, too, but because they are really holes, they can be easily torn apart.

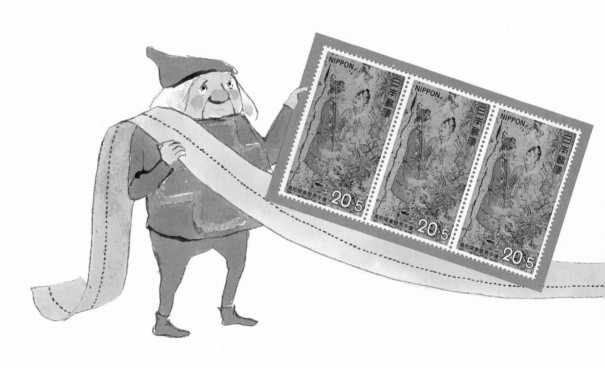

The ants have found a cookie. Lined up to take it home piece by piece, they also look like one long line.

Did you know that pictures may be drawn by lining up dots?
Look at this page up close. You can only see round dots. Now
hold it at a little distance. A strange face appears.

This picture is made by weaving white and black strips of paper. It is the fox in Aesop's fables. Patterns in fabrics are often woven of colored dots and lines like this.

```
                  T · TUTTTTTTTT ·
                  I I UUUTT I TTTTTTTTTTTT · ·
                  · UCCCCUUJUUJ · TTTTTTT I I
                  · CCCSCSJJJJ I · TTTTTTT I T I I I ·
                 · · SSCJSJJUUUUUU I TTTTTTJJ I I I I I I ·
                 · L I I I SSCJJUUUUT TJTTTLLLL I I I · · · ·
                · · VWV · CCJJKSSSSX · CCJJTTTLL I I I I I · · · ·
                E DDWSK · · JJJTSSCX · CJTT I · I I I I I I I I · · · ·
                E DMMWKVS I I JTTCSXF I JJT I · I · I I I I I I · · · ·
                E EDMMWKSS · I JXSSXF I CJTL · I · · I I I I · · · · · ·
                I EDMMMWWK I · JSSEE I C I TL · · L · · L · · JJ I I I · · · ·
                I DMFNWWWK I I · I JSCCC I TL I I · · L · · I I I · · · · · I I
                · KCEHHWWWWBB · I JSSS I CT I TL I I I · · I I I I · · · · I I I
                SKCMHMWWWWW · · I SSSCUU I TT I I · · I I I I I I JVV · · I I S
                SSCEMHMWW · WBM · · SSCCUUTLT I · · · I I I I I LLJV · · I H · I
                I SCEEHMWJLLKB I · · CSSUUSSL · · · I I I I I LJJJJ · · I H · I
                I SCXECCMMCLKWWE · CSSSSS LLC · · I I CCLLLLJJJ I I CLN I
                SCXXECCKJWWBWBB · · · I XSSX LX I LL · · T I I CCLLLLJJJ I CSLN I ·
                SSXXCCKWKKWWB I BB · XXXXLLXJLCJ · I · SCDCCLJJJJLSSN I N ·
                SSMMMWWMMWWWB · I WBS · SSXXXJJC I I I · · · SLSSJJLLLLCSNLN ·
                KSMMWWMC · CWWWK I · BCHK SSSJC I I · · · · I SESESSJCCSJJ ·
                ESMWWMDDWWWWWKWK · BAA CCCLLL · · · · · · JESSJJSSJJ ·
                SSOWWWMDDWWWWWWKKABBASS I I I I I I · · · · · · FS I I · N I I
                SSDDWMMWDDDWWWSWWWBBSJJ I I I I I I I I · · · · FJJ · J I
                SCUWWMMWWOOW · WW · WWWJJJJJ I JJJJ I · · · · TTTTTTVHS · · I
                CUUEWMEEWWWW · WW · MMMWBBSSXXXSKKK I · TUUUUUUUH I A I · ·
                CSUUEEMMOWWWL · · · MMBBWBU · · · XSKKK I · · SS · · · · UHMMVJ I I
                LCU I MEECOOWMMMM · WWWBEEFFTT · SKKK I · · I ATTTFHV I JJ I JJ
                · COO I · EWCWWWWWM · WWWEEEETJ I T · SKKVV · · AAJJJ I BWWMMLLL
                CCOOEEW · CCWWWWVWTEEEEEEETJ I · T I EEVV · · JUUUU · I KWWNNNL
                · I · I SEEEEECCCWWWWEEEEEEELL I · I EEUUV · I · · · · · WWLNLN
                I SSSSEWE I WWWW · BEEEEEBBB · · I JJNEENN I L I TTTTJ I WNNLLL
                SSSSEEWWVSCWWS · FFULUFFF I I JJNFEEUU I L · JJJJ I BBWFFN
                SSSSWWWW I SCCSS · FFULJUUU I I I LNFEEUU I L · I J · I I I B · · U
                SSSSWWWWWWWWWBFFFUUJJ I I I I JJFFEEUU I L I I I I I I I JLAUUU
                SCCEWWWWWWSSASUUJJ I I I JJJFFEEUU L I I I I I I JULASSS
                CCCEWEWEW I I WSSASUUJJ I I JJJ I FEEEUU I V · I I I I I JUUMMMJ
                · CSEWWWEW I WSSSWASUUUUJJJJL I I EWEFFFFJ · I I JJUUMANJ
                CEEEEWCEEWSSSWSSSUUUJJJJ I I AWWWWWWK · I JJJUUNNJ
                SSEECSWWWSSSWWRSSUUUJJJ I FWWWWWWWV · I JUUUENN
                CCSWCSWWWSSSWWRRSSSUUUKAAAAAAAK · JJJJUUEEA
                · SWCSWSSSSSSWWRRSSUUU I I AAAAAANJ I I JJJUFFAA
                · · CWCWWSSSSSSRRMRSSUUUFEFFNJ I J I I I JJJUUU
                CCWWWWSSSSSFFMMRSUUUFEFFU · · JU · JUUUU
                CEWWWSSSFFFFMMRSUUUFEFWWMNUMMMUUUJ
                LEW · SSSSFSMMMRSEEEAWWWWWWNMMMSSU
                · EW · OOSSFSRWWRSEE · WWSSSSCCCUCSSS
                · UU · · OSSFFFFWMRSCSWWEEEEEFFNCSS
                UUU · · OOFFFFEWMSCCCUWWWWWWNCSSS
                UUU · I I OOFFFEEEWMSSSTTTTT I TCUSS
                I I U · · I UOOBFFEEEEWWMSSUU I I I I CSS
                TTLL · · I OOOOSFEEEEEMWSSUU I I I UUSN
                TTEA · I I OOOBWFEEEEEEEWWKSSUUUUUN
                I STTEWJJ I OOBBWWEEEEEEEWWKKEEEEE
                I I STTEW I UFFFBBWWWWEEEEEWWWWWWSL
                JJFFCCEWWUFFEBBWWWWWWEEEEEEEWWWUSL
                JJEE · FFEWWUFFEBBWWWWWWWWWWWWWNUUSL
                JJEEKCCFFWWUFFEBBWWWWWWWWWWWWWUUUSL
                JJJEECCCCFWWUNNEEBWWWWWWWWWWUUUUSL
                I JLFEELLLCSWWUNNEEBWWWWWWWBESUUUUSU
                JKKLET I I I USWWWJEEEBEWWWWWWWBESSUUUUSUU
                I COOEFT I I I SWWWUFFEEBWWWWWWWBESUUUUUSSUU
                I I COFTF I I I I SWWEUFFEBBWWWWWWWBBESUUUUUUSUUU
                I I I JFEFFF I I SSSSSSSFEBEBWWWBBESUUUUUUUSSUUU
                I I I JTTFFFFSSSSSSSSFFEBEBBBBESUUUUUUUUUUUSUUSS
                I I JTT USSSSSUUUUFFEEBBBWBEEUUUUUUUUUUUUUSSULL
                I I TTTU SOSSSOUUUUUSSEEEEUUUUUUUUUUUUUSSULLL
                TTT OOUUUUUUUUUUUUUUUUUUUUUUUUUUSSULULL
                     UUUUUUUUUUUUUUUUUUUUUUUUUUUUSUUUUU I
                     UUJJJJJJJJJUUUUUUUUUSUSSUOO I I
                     JJJJJJJJJUUUUUUUUSSSOO I
                     JJJJJJJJJUUUUUSSS I
                     JJJJJJJJJJJJ I I I I
                     JJJJ
```

One of our little friends made this face by typing letters on a typewriter.

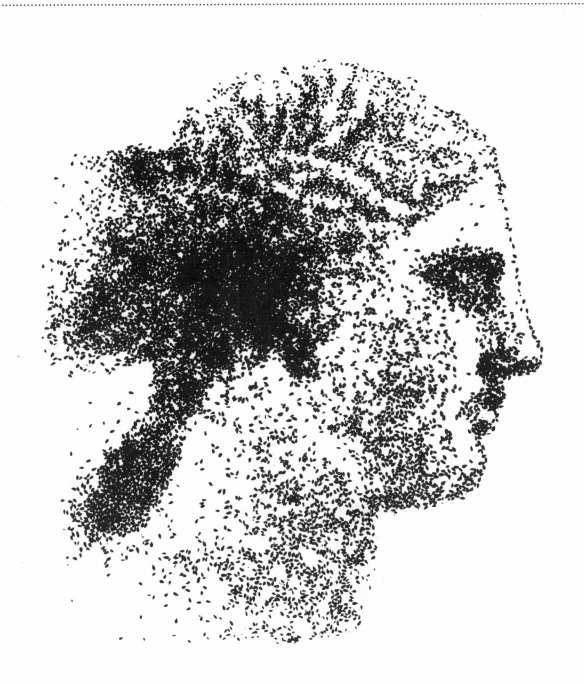

Little black sesame seeds can be eaten. But each seed is also a dot. This picture was made by arranging the seeds.

Using a pen point, the artist has created many dots to make this picture. It is similar to the sesame seed picture that we saw on the last page. Look at your own photograph under a magnifying glass. It too is made of very small dots.

Kriss is doing embroidery called cross-stitch. He is sewing tiny crosses, one by one, using different colored thread. Each cross is like one small dot. But if many of them are put together, they look like a painting. This is a picture of Hans Christian Andersen's story, "The Little Match Girl."

Our little friends are once again using a needle and thread. This time they are putting beads tightly together to make a picture. Completed, it is a picture of a prince riding on a rooster.

If you look at pictures in books or magazines under a magnifying glass, you will see that they are made of many tiny dots. This is an enlarged view of a part of page 52 of this book as seen under a magnifying glass.

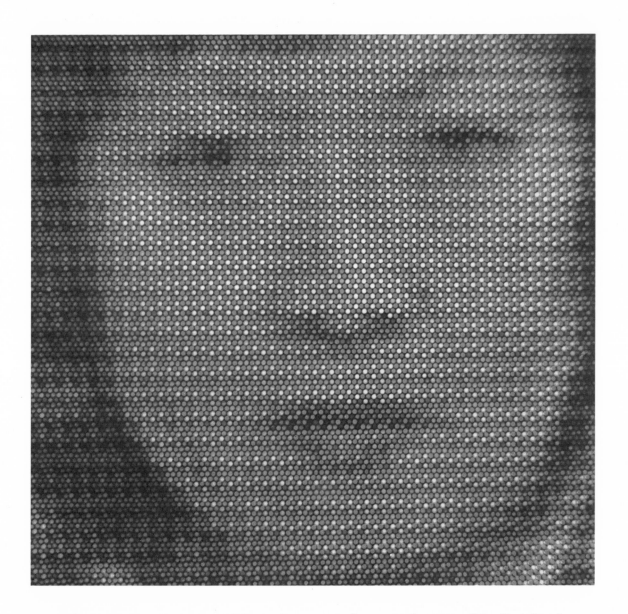

The picture on your TV screen is also made up of individual dots. Look at it for a moment with a magnifying glass. You will see thousands of dots lined up, shining red, blue, and green.

If a picture is divided into parts like the tiles on a bathroom wall, it can be easily copied, part by part. We can think of each part as a dot, then copy it into its own place.

There are many, many things that are made of collections of dots, so let's look for them. As a matter of fact, everything in the world, including human beings, is made of millions of dots assembled together. These dots are called atoms.

# ·4·

# Counting With Circles

Here are some children.

Let's draw a picture of them.

Let's make it simpler.

Now a little simpler.

Even more simple…

The children are now just little circles.

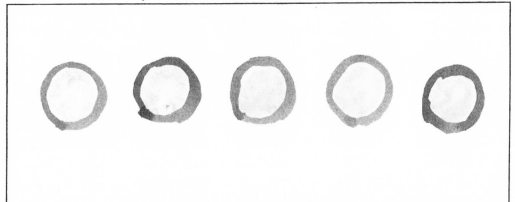

Now let's draw the horses.

A little simpler…

until the horses are just little circles.

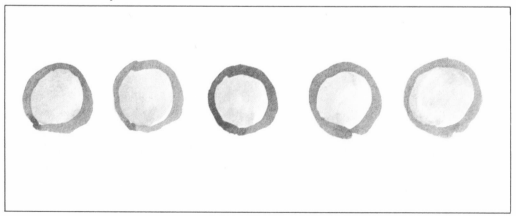

Now let's make both the horses and the children into little circles.

Here they are.

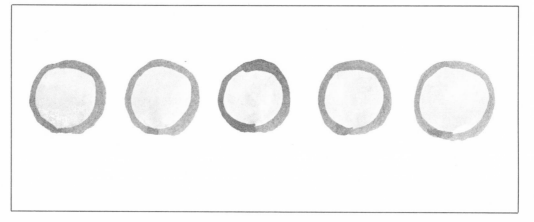

We can make anything we want into little circles:

The big elephants,          the little ants,          the lovely flowers.

Look, they all have the same number of circles.

the tall, tall trees,          the flying birds,          the little bird houses.

Look at these pictures from left to right.

The bird cage
is full.

Now there are
this many.

Now three...

This time look at the pictures from right to left.

Two...

Then one bird.

The cage is empty.

Now see if you can figure out what these circles represent.

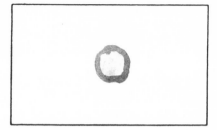 

Match the circle or sets of circles to the different things in the picture below.

  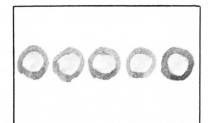

What do these circles represent in the scene below?

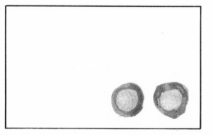

Do you see what our little friends are doing? They're making the little circles into squares so they can pile them up. That's so they'll be easier to count.

# Each number has a name and symbol which stands for the number.

Now you don't need little circles.

0

This number is 1.

1

This number is 2.

2

This number is 6.

6

This number is 7.

7

When you write the number symbol, it makes counting easier.

This number is 3.

3

This number is 4.

4

This number is 5.

5

This number is 8.

8

This number is 9.

9

This number is.... Uh-oh, this square won't fit.

Kriss and Kross have taken
the row of squares and tied
them together. Now they can
put them into the warehouse
next door. The number is 10.

1 0

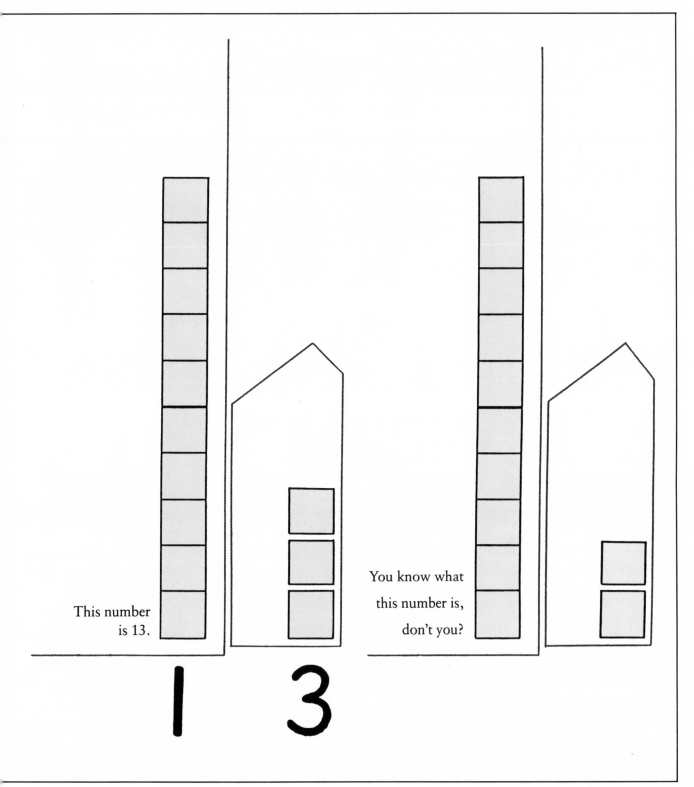

This number is 13.

You know what this number is, don't you?

1  3

It's your turn to count. Can you write the numbers?

| horses | 3 |
| butterflies | 8 |
| foxes | 1 |
| snails | 6 |
| flowers | 9 |
| children | 5 |
| mice | 7 |
| squirrels | 2 |
| trees | 4 |
| little birds | 10 |

Let's try again!
How many of each
thing is there this
time?

| | |
|---|---|
| horses | 4 |
| butterflies | 9 |
| foxes | 2 |
| snails | 5 |
| flowers | 8 |
| children | 6 |
| mice | 10 |
| squirrels | 1 |
| trees | 4 |
| little birds | 12 |

# · 5 ·

# Counting Water

Kross is trying to count these peas. "What a bother!" he says. "It would take years to count them all!"

In the last chapter we counted children and horses by making them little circles.  Counting by making things into little circles is fine, but how can we possibly count so many peas?

What about salt or sugar? There are too many grains to count in that way. And what about water? Can you think of another way to count salt or water?

If we put some salt or water into containers like this, at least we have a way to compare. We can see which container has more water in it.

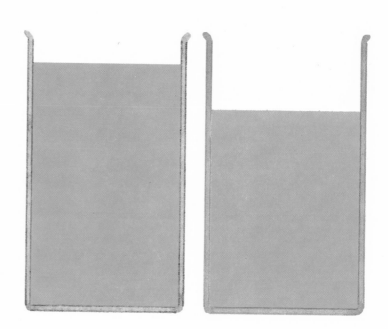

Look at these containers. Which one has more water in it?

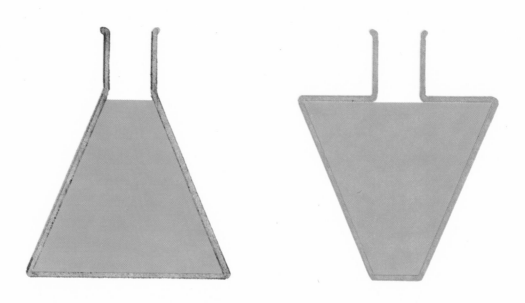

How about these?

We can't tell which of these containers has more water in it just by looking, can we?

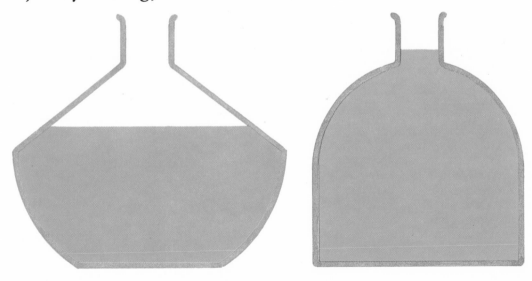

If we can't tell just by looking, we can pour the water into other containers that are the same size and shape. But we still can't write down in numbers just how much more water one container has than the other.

Well then, let's try putting the water into smaller cups. Now we can see that the pink container had two more cups of water than the green container. We call counting this way "measuring." When we measure liquids like water, the container we use is called a "measure."

When we use little cups as measures,
it's hard to measure exactly.

So what shall we do when
there's a little left over, like
this? We could say we have
four cups plus a little. But
that doesn't tell us much, so

we need to agree on a rule.
If there's more than half, we'll say it's one cup.
If there's exactly half, we'll still say it's a cup.
If there's less than half, we'll say there's none.

Take a look at these measures.
Using our rule, which would you say are "full"?
Which are "empty"?

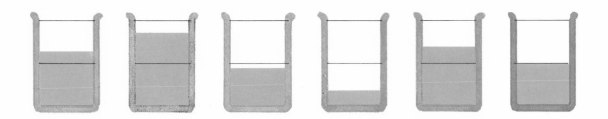

Our little friends used cups to measure
the water in a great big washbowl.
"This is just like counting peas! How
bothersome!"

Then our friends
had an idea. They took
ten cups and tied them together
so they could measure
all at once.

Then they thought up
some other "measures."

And finally,
hit upon
the best one yet.

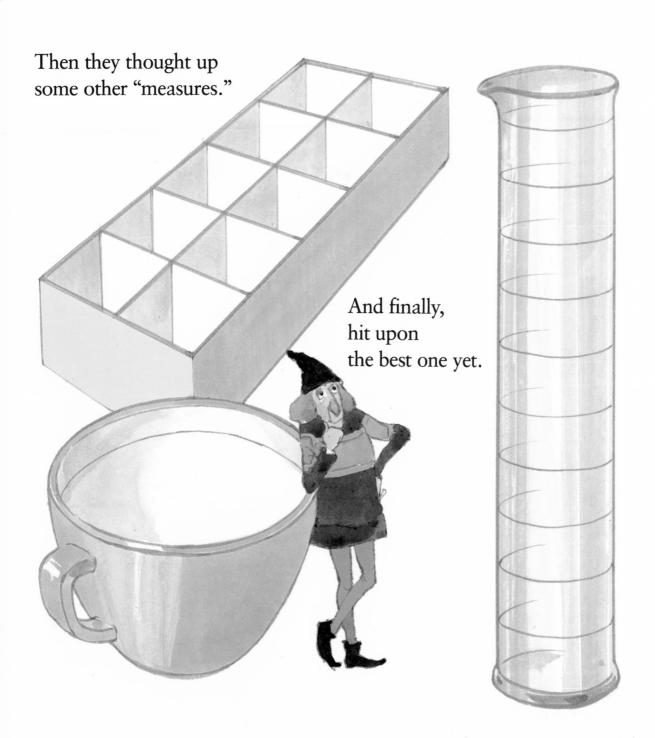

This kind of measure was really handy. When they measured the water from the washbowl again, they counted 68 cups.

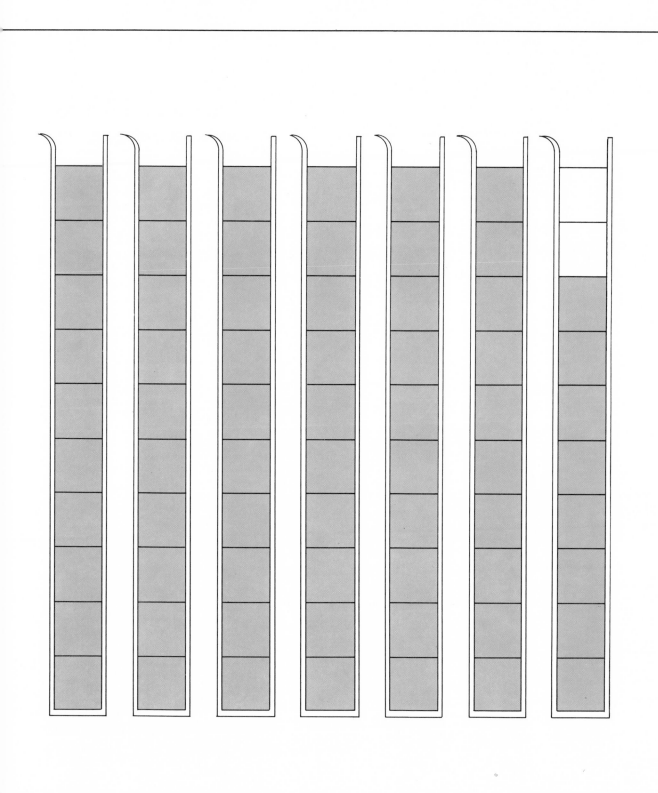

Our friends measured water from all different kinds of containers in this way. How many cups did each contain?

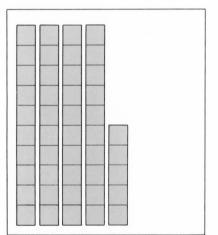

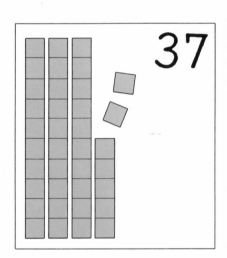

37

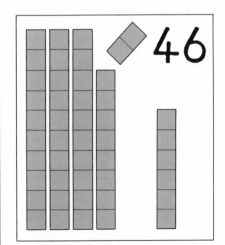

46

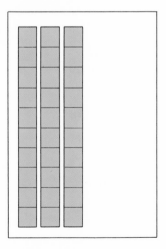

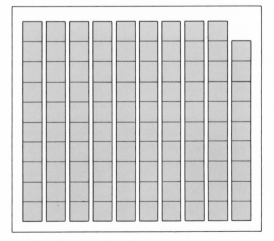

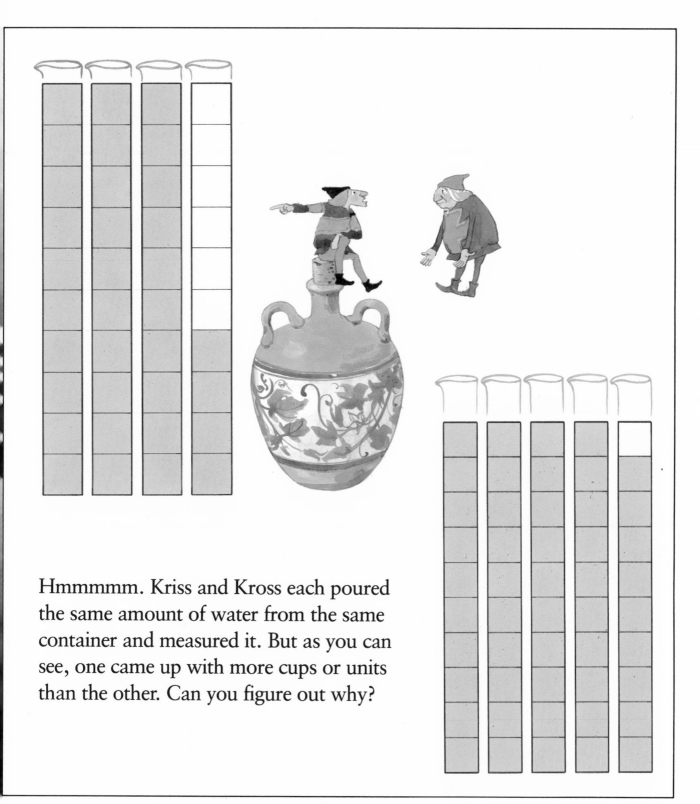

Hmmmmm. Kriss and Kross each poured the same amount of water from the same container and measured it. But as you can see, one came up with more cups or units than the other. Can you figure out why?

If the size of the "measure" that you use is not the same as someone else's, you simply can't compare. That's why everyone all over the world has agreed to use the measures that you see here.

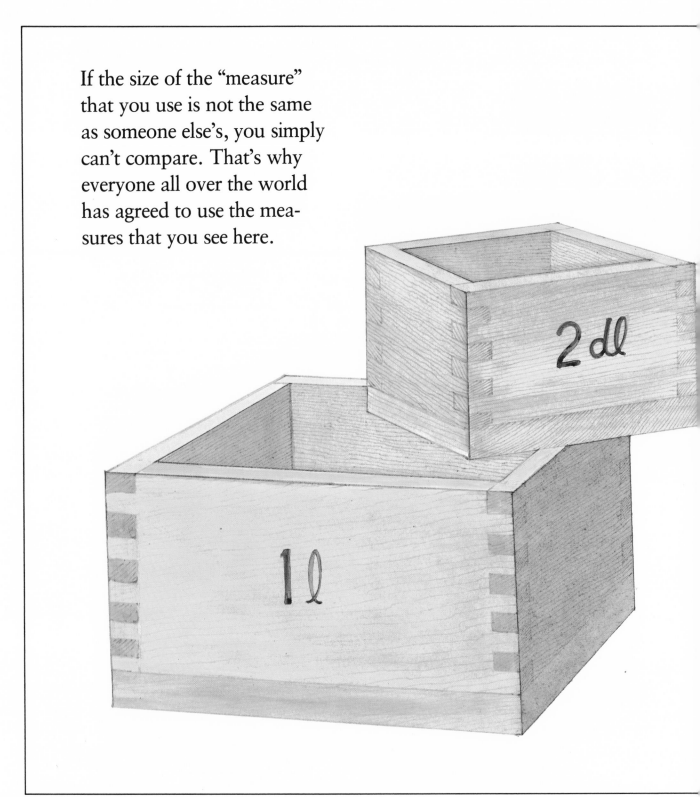

Have you ever seen "measures" like this before? Perhaps, like Kriss and Kross, you are using them already.

# Afterword

## 1 · The Magic Machine

Have you ever washed the windows, stood back to admire their gleaming brightness, and then immediately afterwards it began to rain? Didn't you suspect, despite all reason, that the washing of the windows *caused* the rain? There seemed to be a cause and effect relationship between one event and the other.

We live in a world of seemingly magical machines. We have machines that give us coffee, or candy, or newspapers when we put coins into their slots. We have machines that wash or dry our clothes, and machines that raise barriers and allow us to drive across bridges when we put the exact change into them. The idea of putting something into a machine and having something different come out is very familiar to us.

We put money into a bank account and it has interest added when we take it out. This is not a mechanical device, but there is a fixed relationship between what is put in and what comes out.

This chapter explores the idea of relationships. There is a relationship between things on the right page and things on the left. The machine is used to symbolize the relationship.

We often use the word "relationship." It is an abstraction for something that no one has ever seen, but that everyone can understand.

Parent and child, doctor and patient, iron and magnets, 6 and 3—when we consider two things together, we realize that this strange thing called a relationship binds them together.

It is somewhat easier to express the relationship between two numbers, since we have symbols to show the nature of the relationship. For example, the number ½, besides meaning half of 1, or one divided by two, also shows the relationship itself. So we can use the same symbol (/) to show the relationship between 3 and 6 (3/6), or 50 and 100 (50/100).

Because "relationship" is a concept that exists only in our minds, not in the real world, we can use the notion of the magic machine to represent this concept. In a way the machine is like our minds, which can imagine or fantasize all sorts of connections. Unlike this machine, which has limits, the world inside our minds has unlimited possibilities. For example, if, as in the opening example, we make the washing of the windows the "cause" and the rain the "effect," we are not drawing a scientifically supported conclusion. Our minds are broken like the broken magic machine at the end of the first chapter. If this imaginative kind of thinking is scientifically supported, however, the observation may serve as a foothold for creative new thought. Although not very scientific, these connections can be the beginning of developing imaginative and creative power. It is the ability to engage in such relationship-seeking that enables imaginative problem solving to take place.

## 2 · Compare and Find Out

Skill in comparing things for likenesses and differences is, like formulating relationships, basic to the ability to solve problems. Indeed, it is the basis of all scientific thinking. This skill is necessary for making decisions in our everyday lives.

We compare items to be purchased, for example: two suits cost the same, but one has better fabric; they have the same design and fabric, but one is on sale; they have the same design, fabric, and cost, but one comes with free alterations.

Comparing involves thinking about the differences, but also requires looking for similarities. If we establish what two pictures or events have in common, the differences often reveal themselves. In casual, everyday situations, there are many instances in which we make comparisons: who is winning the race; which trail up the mountain is the best; how should we portion the juice. Almost all mathematics are based on making comparisons. In fact, if word problems can be considered in terms of comparisons, they are easier to solve. An example from the mathematics of upper grades can illustrate this:

> If a gold chain is put on a watch, the cost is \$1,550. If the chain is silver, it costs \$1,390. If we simply buy one gold chain and one silver chain, their total cost would be \$540. How much is the watch?

As long as it is possible to compare one thing at a time, in many cases we can find the differences, even with pictures as intricate as those on pages 32 and 33. However, the pictures on pages 26 through 33 are identical if we compare one part at a time; it is only in regarding them as a whole that we find the difference. Striving to describe, in their own words, these somewhat subtle differences can help children think more precisely about what they observe.

In this chapter I have given examples of a great variety of differences: quantity, size, arrangement, type, position, elements. Unfortunately, the limits of the printed page restricts us to two-dimensional figures. It would be a good idea to have children explore the differences and similarities among three-dimensional objects.

## 3 · Dots, Dots, and More Dots

I couldn't help being reminded of the impressionists while writing *Dots, Dots, and More Dots.*

During the latter part of the nineteenth century, scientific inventions and discoveries followed one after the other. Research in the optical sciences brought about a new concept of color. At the same time, Monet led the way to a revolutionary new style of painting that also established new ways of using color. Unlike the somberness of earlier western paintings, pastoral scenes seen through impressionist eyes sparkled with sunlight. Instead of mixing the paint on the palette, dots of primary color were put directly on the canvas and "mixed in the retina of the beholder." This was also the theory of the pointillists, who emerged from among the impressionists. *Sunday Afternoon on the Island of La Grande Jatte* by Seurat is an especially famous pointillist painting. It is very interesting that this new painting style should appear at the same time as the dawning of the scientific age.

I hope to draw your attention to the fact that many of the things that we casually observe in the everyday world are made up of countless points. I am not talking so much about the "point" as defined by mathematicians, but the point we use in everyday language, a tiny dot: the point we would use to describe a large star seen from a great distance.

All of the examples in this book were made by human beings, but the natural world provides many examples of things made of tiny parts or "points," such as the scales on a butterfly's wing or the kernels on an ear of corn.

But that is not all. All matter in the universe is made up of points. Since the time of the ancient Greeks, people have been trying to discover what the structure of matter is. It is only recently, at the beginning of this century, that physicists developed the concept of elementary particles: atoms, electrons, neutrons, among them.

The size of an atom is about one hundred-millionth of a centimeter, so it is impossible to see one with the naked eye. But the discovery of this minuscule particle has not only caused the rewriting of 2,000 years of physics, but has changed our society and our way of thinking. When we take a new look at our world with these minute points in mind, it will appear new and fresh.

Using the concept of the point can change our thinking as well. It can also be used to solve problems. An example of this is to analyze something into minuscule dots, as we have done in this chapter. On page 53 the original picture is partitioned into a graph. Each partition can be considered a point. If you copy the points as shown by the co-ordinates, you can copy the picture quite accurately. This is an example of analytical thinking.

## 4 · Counting With Circles

Helen Keller writes in her biography, "The most meaningful, precious day of my life was the day Miss Sullivan came to my home."

It was around the time of the blind Helen's seventh birthday. Miss Sullivan, her teacher, wrote D-O-L-L on Helen's palm, while making her touch a doll. Helen soon memorized this. But she was only memorizing—she did not understand that they were letters or that there was a word "doll." She had no idea whether these taps on her hand had to do with this particular doll, or whether they could be used for other dolls as well.

Dirt, water, mother—Helen learned the name of each thing her hand touched. It must have been difficult for her at first to store these meaningless symbols in her memory.

In the movie *The Miracle Worker*, when the naughty Helen runs recklessly and falls into a stream, Miss Sullivan writes W-A-T-E-R on her palm, while Helen is still standing in the stream. Previously, when the maid had given her some water to drink, when Helen's hand touched the water in the well, and now, when the two of them stood soaking wet in the stream, Miss Sullivan wrote the same symbol W-A-T-E-R on Helen's palm. At this point, Helen discovered that this is a symbol meaning water. Suddenly it dawned on her that the symbols that Miss Sullivan had been teaching her over a long period of time, such as water or mother or tree, were words with meanings. Helen pounded the ground, rubbed her cheeks on it, and cried as she wrote "earth" on the ground. It was an ecstatic moment.

The affection and enthusiasm of Miss Sullivan cannot be denied, but from the time that Helen grasped that ideas could be expressed through words, she was able to make her own way into the world of understanding through the power of words and letters. She learned to speak!

I thought of Helen Keller as I worked on this book. Children often count out loud. There are even child prodigies who can count to several hundred thousand. But, like the symbols that were written on Helen's hand, these are learned by rote and have no relation to the understanding of math.

There are ○○○○○ flowers, ○○○○○ people, ○○○○○ dogs; the symbol "5" expresses this idea. When children discover this concept, the 5 moves around freely in their minds, an abstraction no longer tied to a particular set of things. How wonderful it would be if children could grasp this idea with the same excitement as when Helen Keller discovered the meaning of water.

## 5 · Counting Water

What do you think of this statement: "Two clay balls the same size are combined to make one ball. We can write this as an equation: $1 + 1 = 1$."

What is wrong with this thinking?

There are two kinds of quantity. First, there are things like people and apples that can be counted one by one, and that lose their original shape when divided in two. This is called "discrete quantity." The second kind of quantity involves things like water and sugar, which can't be counted one by one, or time and distance, which go on and on. This is called "indiscrete" or "continuous" quantity. Continuous quantity is measured by being matched to (or contained in) a unit of measure.

The problem cited earlier caused confusion because clay has the properties of a continuous quantity, yet when it is formed into a ball it has the properties of a discrete property as well. Clay balls can, of course, be counted discretely, but must be measured like a continuous quantity, when gathered together into one ball. In order to avoid confusion, we must agree on what to use as a unit of measurement.

The theme of this chapter is measuring water by using a small cup as the unit. To measure is to count in units. I would like the reader to actually measure water, not just look at the book. Remember that liter (l) is the universal unit when measuring volume. One liter contains 1,000 cubic centimeters ($cm^3$), centimeter being a unit of length.

One day in the summer of 1792, a team of French surveyors, lugging signals and reflective mirrors, crossed into Spain. No doubt people in the area looked at them suspiciously and demanded, "What on earth have you come here to do?" Their answer would have been: "We've come to measure the meridian. We want to measure the distance around the earth, and make a unit of length based on it." Who at that time would have believed them?

In the eighteenth century each country and even each district had its own units of measure, which made it very confusing to travel or trade from one place to another. The French Academy wanted to create a fixed unit that would be used universally. Their idea was to take one ten-millionth of the line from the equator to the pole, and call it one meter. The Academy proposed to all the world to measure the earth, since it was the commonest property of all humankind, the largest and most stable thing in existence. Wasn't that a wonderful idea?

When you think that this unit we call 1 meter was based not on the height of some conqueror or on the length of some building, but on an aspect of this irreplaceable entity called Earth, doesn't it make you feel connected to our amazing universe?

MITSUMASA ANNO is known the world over for his highly original and thought-provoking picture books, and in 1984 he was awarded the Hans Christian Andersen Prize, the highest honor attainable in the field of children's book illustration. A man of many talents and interests, Mr. Anno shares his enthusiasm for art, nature, history, literature, mathematics, travel and people with young readers through his uniquely imaginative books. He feels that the mathematical laws that underlie nature are as beautiful as other aspects of the wonderful world we live in, and that even very small children can understand and appreciate them if they are clearly and appealingly presented. In this book, which offers very young children a learning experience that is as enjoyable as a game, he demonstrates his belief that mathematics is more than merely manipulating numbers, it is a way of thinking, and that it has bearing on all scholastic subjects, indeed on all forms of creative thought. Born in 1926 in Tsuwano, in Western Japan, Mr. Anno is a graduate of the Yamaguchi Teacher Training College and worked for some time as a teacher before becoming an artist. He now lives in Tokyo, but he travels all over the world to do research for his many books.

*Other Books by Mitsumasa Anno*
*published by Philomel Books*

All In A Day

Anno's Animals

Anno's Britain

Anno's Counting House

Anno's Faces

Anno's Flea Market

Anno's Hat Tricks

Anno's Italy

Anno's Journey

Anno's Magical ABC:
An Anamorphic Alphabet

Anno's Mysterious Multiplying Jar

Anno's Peekaboo

Anno's Sundial

Anno's U.S.A.

The King's Flower

Socrates And The
Three Little Pigs

The Unique World of Mitsumasa Anno:
Selected Works (1969–1977)

The publishers would like to thank Joan Oltman
for her help in the translation
and preparation of this book.

*Anno's Math Games II* by Mitsumasa Anno, copyright ©1982 by Kuso Kobo,
first published in 1982 by Fukuinkan Shoten Publishers, Inc., Tokyo. Translation
and special contents of this edition copyright ©1989 by Philomel Books, and first
published in 1989 by Philomel Books, a division of The Putnam & Grosset Group,
200 Madison Avenue, New York, NY 10016. Published simultaneously in
Canada. All rights reserved. Printed in Japan.

Library of Congress Cataloging-in-Publication Data (Revised for vol. 2) Anno,
Mitsumasa, 1926- Anno's math games. Translation of: Hajimete deau sūgaku no
ehon. Summary: Picture puzzles, games, and simple activities introduce the mathematical concepts of multiplication, sequence, and ordinal numbering, measurement, and direction. 1. Mathematical recreations—Juvenile literature.
[1. Mathematical recreations. 2. Picture puzzles] I. Title. II. Title: Math
games. QA95.A5613 1987 793.7'4 86-30513 ISBN 0-399-21151-9
(Volume I) ISBN 0-399-21615-4 (Volume II)

BOMC offers recordings compact discs, cassettes
and records. For information and catalog write to
BOMR, Camp Hill, PA 17012.